NINJA CREAMI DELUXE VEGAN COOKBOOK

40+ healthy homemade plant-based, dairy-free, gluten-free, low-calories frozen desserts recipes to enjoy ice cream treats for every occasion

BECK C. BLAKES

COPYRIGHT

DISCLAIMER

The recipes and information contained in this book are for general guidance only and are not intended to be medical or nutritional advice. Before making any changes to your diet or cooking habits, please consult a qualified healthcare professional or registered dietitian. Nutritional information is approximate and may vary based on specific ingredients and portion sizes. Some recipes may include ingredients that are common allergens or may not be suitable for everyone. Please follow proper food handling and cooking guidelines to ensure food safety. By using this book, you agree to hold harmless the author, publisher, and any other parties involved in the creation and distribution of this book from any damages or liabilities resulting from your use of the recipes and information contained herein."

TABLE OF CONTENTS

INTRODUCTION

INTRODUCTION

Have you ever dreamed of diving into a bowl of creamy, decadent ice cream that's not only delicious but also aligns with your values and dietary choices? Look no further. The "Ninja Creami Deluxe Vegan Cookbook" is here to make your dreams come true, one scoop at a time.

Why Vegan?

Choosing a vegan lifestyle is more than just a trend—it's a commitment to better health, compassion for animals, and a positive impact on the environment. But let's be honest, finding truly indulgent vegan desserts can be a challenge. That's where this cookbook steps in, transforming the way you think about vegan ice cream.

The Sweet Benefits of Going Vegan with Ninja Creami

1. **Healthier Indulgence**: Imagine enjoying your favorite ice cream flavors without the guilt. Our vegan recipes are made with wholesome, plant-based ingredients that nourish your body. You'll feel great knowing you're indulging in a treat that's free from dairy and packed with nutrients.
2. **Compassionate Choices**: Every recipe in this book is 100% cruelty-free. By choosing vegan ice cream, you're making a stand for animal welfare and embracing a more compassionate way of living. It's ice cream you can feel good about.
3. **Eco-Friendly Delights**: Did you know that a vegan diet has a lower carbon footprint compared to a diet that includes animal products? By making these delicious vegan treats, you're contributing to a healthier planet. Enjoy your ice cream knowing you're helping to reduce your environmental impact.

4. **Allergen-Friendly**: Many people struggle with lactose intolerance or other dairy-related allergies. Vegan ice cream is naturally free from common allergens, making it a safe and delightful choice for everyone. Now, everyone at the table can enjoy dessert without worry.

Why You'll Love the Ninja Creami Deluxe Vegan Cookbook

- **Diverse Flavors**: From classic vanilla bean to exotic matcha green tea, this cookbook is bursting with flavors that cater to every palate. You won't believe how creamy and delicious vegan ice cream can be!
- **Easy and Fun**: You don't need to be a kitchen pro to make these recipes. We've laid out each step clearly, so you can whip up your favorite treats with ease. Plus, using the Ninja Creami is a breeze—clean-up included.
- **Community of Like-Minded Enthusiasts**: When you buy this book, you're not just getting recipes. You're joining a vibrant community of vegan ice cream lovers. Share your creations, find inspiration, and connect with others who share your passion for delicious, ethical desserts.

Get Ready to Scoop Happiness

With the "Ninja Creami Deluxe Vegan Cookbook," you're not just making ice cream; you're embracing a lifestyle that's healthier, kinder, and more sustainable. Whether you're already vegan or just curious about plant-based eating, this book is your perfect companion on the journey to creamy, dreamy desserts.

So, why wait? Treat yourself to the best vegan ice cream you've ever tasted. Click the "Buy Now" button and start creating delicious memories today. Your taste buds—and the planet—will thank you.

WHAT IS NINJA CREAMI DELUXE?

The Ninja Creami Deluxe is a cutting-edge ice cream maker designed for effortlessly creating homemade frozen treats. I use mine almost daily and appreciate its powerful motor and unique blending technology that turn ingredients into smooth ice creams, sorbets, and frozen yogurts. Just add your chosen ingredients, select a program, and let the Ninja Creami Deluxe handle the rest. In no time, you'll have delicious homemade ice cream to enjoy.

Vegan Ninja Creami Deluxe Recipes: Plant-Based Ice Creams

These vegan Ninja Creami Deluxe ice cream recipes demonstrate that dairy-free desserts can be as satisfying and delicious as traditional ones. Say goodbye to the limitations of store-bought options and unleash your creativity with the Ninja Creami Deluxe. With its user-friendly design and endless possibilities, you'll enjoy homemade vegan ice cream like never before.

CLEANING THE NINJA CREAMI DELUXE

Cleaning the Ninja Creami Deluxe is a breeze. The machine features a detachable bowl and paddle, which can be easily cleaned with warm soapy water. Use a damp cloth to wipe down the machine's body. Both the bowl and paddle are dishwasher-safe. Before using the machine again, ensure that the bowl and paddle are completely dry, as any remaining moisture can affect the consistency of your frozen treats.

MAINTAINING THE NINJA CREAMI DELUXE

To prevent buildup of ice cream or other frozen treats, wipe down the machine after each use. Regularly check the machine's motor and other parts for signs of wear. The instruction manual recommends applying food-grade silicone lubrication to the motor shaft for smooth operation. Additionally, it's a good idea to regularly tighten any loose screws or nuts.

 FAQ

1. What is vegan ice cream made of?
Vegan ice cream can be created using various plant-based milk alternatives, including soy, oat, almond, and coconut milk.

2. Does vegan ice cream taste the same?
The taste of vegan ice cream can vary depending on the ingredients used. You might detect flavors from the coconut, almond, or other milk alternatives, but typically, stronger flavors like chocolate, fruit, and caramel will dominate.

3. What's the difference between vegan and dairy-free?
A vegan diet excludes all animal products. Therefore, vegan ice cream is not only free of dairy, such as milk and cream, but also avoids eggs, honey, gelatin, and certain additives processed with animal products.

4. How can I make my vegan ice cream more creamy?
For creamier vegan ice cream, aim for a thick base. Coconut milk is generally richer than other plant-based milks, but avoid the low-fat variety. You can also enhance creaminess by adding thickeners like cashew cream, coconut cream, or even avocado.

5. What substitutes can I use to make other ice cream recipes dairy-free?
To make ice cream recipes dairy-free for those with lactose intolerance, you can substitute unsweetened oat milk for regular milk (1:1), unsweetened coconut cream for double cream (1:1), and vegan cream cheese for traditional cream cheese (1:1).

6. Is vegan ice cream better for you?

Dairy-free ice cream can have lower levels of saturated fat and cholesterol compared to traditional dairy ice cream. However, they may still contain significant amounts of sugar from sources like fruit or added toppings. For a lighter treat, consider options like zesty fruit sorbets or "nice creams" made entirely from frozen fruits like bananas. Remember, desserts should be consumed in moderation as part of a balanced diet.

7. Vegan-friendly toppings and mix-ins

Enhance your dessert with vegan-friendly toppings such as vegan sweets, vegan biscuits, or nuts for added texture and crunch. You can crush them and sprinkle them on top for a sumptuous sundae, or use the Ninja CREAMi 'Mix-Ins' program to distribute them evenly throughout your tub for a delightful surprise in every bite.

8. What vegan sweets and vegan biscuits are there?

The growing popularity of plant-based diets has made dairy-free and vegan sweets and biscuits more accessible in UK shops. Options range from well-known brands to supermarket-own ranges, including gelatin-free marshmallows and gummy sweets, vegan speculoos cookies, dairy-free dark chocolate chunks, and much more. Experiment to discover your favorites!

TIPS FOR CREATING VEGAN NINJA CREAMI DELUXE ICE CREAM

1. **The Key Ingredients for Successful Vegan Ice Cream:** The base of vegan ice cream is typically a plant-based milk alternative, such as almond, soy, oat, or coconut milk. These milks provide a creamy texture and subtle sweetness while being free of dairy products. To have better control over the sugar content, it is advisable to choose an unsweetened option.

2. **Natural Sweetener:** To sweeten your vegan ice cream, consider using natural sweeteners like agave syrup. It provides a delicate sweetness and is less likely to cause blood sugar spikes compared to refined sugars.

3. **Natural and Intense Flavors:** One advantage of vegan ice cream is the opportunity to experiment with a variety of natural flavors. For fruity ice creams, use fresh, ripe fruit. To achieve rich, complex flavors, add ingredients like pure vanilla extract, unsweetened cocoa powder, or nut purees.

4. **Vegan Mix-ins: Nuts, Nuggets, and More:** Vegan ice creams are perfect for adding healthy and delicious mix-ins. Chopped nuts, vegan dark chocolate chips, dried fruit, and even vegan cookie pieces are great choices for adding texture and flavor to your frozen creations.

5. **The Creamy Texture: Tips for Success:** To achieve a creamy texture in your vegan ice cream, make sure to mix the ingredients well until they are smooth and consistent. Adding thick coconut cream can enhance the richness and creaminess of the texture.

6. **Maximum Customization: Your Own Vegan Recipes:** One of the joys of creating vegan ice cream is the customization. You can try different flavors, spices, and add-ins to make recipes that are uniquely yours. Try adding cinnamon to apple ice cream, salted caramel chips to peanut butter ice cream, or orange zest to dark chocolate ice cream.

7. **Vegan Sorbet: Dairy-Free Refreshment:** Vegan sorbets offer a light and refreshing option. You can make them with fresh fruit and water, sweetened with a little agave syrup for a subtle sweetness. Sorbets are perfect for hot days or as a refreshing end to a hearty meal.

8. **Savor the Creaminess of Vegan Ice Cream:** Enjoy incredibly creamy vegan ice cream guilt-free, thanks to plant-based milk bases and expert preparation techniques. Explore the diversity of flavors and ingredients that deliver a creamy texture, allowing you to indulge in vegan ice creams that are just as rich and satisfying as their dairy-based counterparts.

9. **Conservation and Tasting:** Vegan ice creams tend to have a slightly different texture than dairy-based ice creams, but they are just as delicious. Be sure to store your creations in

the freezer and let them soften slightly before serving for optimal texture.

- **Experiment with Superfoods:** Incorporate superfoods like spirulina powder, matcha powder, or chia seeds for even more nutritious vegan ice cream.

HOW TO PREPARE A TREAT

- First, create your recipe and Pour the base mixture into an empty CREAMi Deluxe Pint and cover it with a storage lid. Then for 24 hours you'll freeze it.

- When you're ready to prepare your dessert. After freezing, remove the pint from the freezer and take off the lid. Place the pint in the outer bowl and attach the Creamerizer Paddle to the lid, securing the lid assembly.
  Position the bowl assembly on the motor base and twist the handle to raise the platform and lock it in place.

- You press a button to indicate whether your cup is full or half-full. If it's half, you can combine the top half of a full cup or what's left over at the bottom. This is great for
  - a) creating two different tastes in one pint and
  - b) recycling leftovers.
  - You scroll the dial to the desired program, such as ice cream or sorbet. You hit the go button.

- For example: Choose- (TOP, FULL, or BOTTOM) - and choose the ICE CREAM setting using the dial.

- It takes roughly two minutes to mix.

- You can then add toppings and flavorings to your liking. If you do add flavors, go back in and hit Add-In.

- After two minutes, your frozen delight is ready.

VEGAN ICE CREAM

Vegan Blackberry Lemon Ice Cream

PREP TIME 15 min. Freeze Time 1 d   SERVINGS 3

INGREDIENTS

First blend

- 1.5 cups (360 ml) nondairy milk
- 1 + 2 tablespoons blackberries (about 6 oz. / 170 grams fresh or frozen)
- 3 tablespoons cashew butter or 1/4 cup (60 ml) soaked cashews (or use 1/2 cup (120 ml) rolled oats to make nut-free)

Second blend

- 3 tablespoons maple syrup or liquid sweetener of your choice to taste or about 3 dates
- 3 teaspoons (15 ml) lemon juice
- 0.75 teaspoon (1.5 grams) lemon zest
- 0.75 teaspoon (3.75 ml) vanilla extract or 1/4 teaspoon (1 gram) vanilla powder

INSTRUCTIONS

1. Combine the water, blackberries, and cashew butter in a blender and blend until smooth, except for the seeds. The seeds may remain but will be strained out in the next step.

2. Pour the blended mixture through a fine-mesh strainer to remove the seeds, and rinse the blender to remove any remaining seeds or pulp.

3. Return the strained mixture to the clean blender and add the sweetener of your choice, lemon juice, zest, and vanilla.

4. Transfer the mixture to a Creami deluxe pint and freeze for 24 hours.

5. Use the lite ice cream setting to spin the mixture.

6. If the mixture is still powdery, use the respin button.

NOTES

- For a refined sugar-free option, substitute 3–4 large dates for the maple syrup; you may need less liquid.

- To make this recipe nut-free, blend in 1/2 cup rolled oats for a thicker, nondairy milk. Alternatively, you can use okara, soymilk pulp, or mashed white sweet potato.

Nutrition Information: SERVING SIZE: 1

Calories: 231kcal   Carbohydrates: 28g   Protein: 7g   Fat: 11g
Fiber: 4g   Sugar: 18g

VEGAN BLUEBERRY MATCHA GREEN TEA ICE CREAM

PREP TIME 10 min. Freeze Time 1 d   SERVINGS 3

INGREDIENTS

- (150 grams) 1 cup blueberries (fresh or frozen)
- 1 cup (240 ml) water
- 3 tablespoons JOI oat milk powder (or use 1 cup plus 3 tablespoons (270 ml) oat milk or oat cream and leave out the water)
- 3 pitted medjool dates
- 1.5 teaspoons (3.75 grams) matcha green tea powder

INSTRUCTIONS

1. Add the blueberries to your Ninja Creami deluxe pint.
2. In a blender, blend the water, JOI oat milk powder, dates, and matcha until smooth.
3. Freeze the mixture for 24 hours on a level surface.
4. After freezing, if there's a hump or volcano, level the top by scraping it with a tablespoon to ensure it's even.
5. Postion the pint into the outer bowl and secure the outer lid.
6. Select the lite ice cream setting to spin the mixture.
7. If the mixture is powdery or crumbly, add a few tablespoons of non-dairy milk and use the respin button. Repeat this step as needed, and add a liquid sweetener if the mixture isn't sweet enough.

8. Level off any leftovers and store in the freezer in the Creami deluxe pint.

9. When ready to eat the leftovers, pull them out and spin on the lite ice cream setting as above.

Nutrition Information: SERVING SIZE: 1

Calories: 160kcal   Carbohydrates: 35g   Protein: 4g   Fat: 2g

VEGAN ELDERFLOWER ICE CREAM

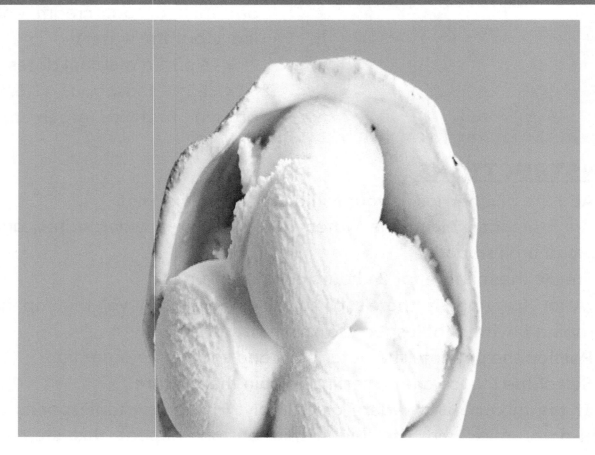

PREP TIME 5 min. Freeze Time 1 d   SERVINGS 4

INGREDIENTS

- 200ml whippable oat cream / 7fl. oz whippable oat cream
- 150ml unsweetened oat milk / 5fl. oz unsweetened oat milk
- 4 tbsp elderflower cordial
- 2 tbsp light agave syrup
- 3 tbsp caster sugar

INSTRUCTIONS

1. In a medium bowl, combine all ingredients and mix until the sugar is dissolved.

2. Pour the mixture into an empty pint, cover with the lid, and freeze for 24 hours.

3. After freezing, remove the pint from the freezer and take off the lid.

4. Select the ICE CREAM setting.

5. Once processing is complete, either add mix-ins or serve the ice cream immediately.

NOTES

- If oat cream and milk are unavailable, you can substitute them with your favorite plant-based whippable cream and milk.

- If your freezer is set to a very cold temperature, the ice cream may appear crumbly. If this happens, select the RE-SPIN setting to process the mixture further.

VEGAN STRAWBERRY ICE CREAM

PREP TIME 5 min. Freeze Time 1 d   SERVINGS 4

INGREDIENTS

- 7.88oz / 225g strawberries, hulled and sliced
- 2.8oz / 80g caster sugar
- 7fl. oz / 200ml soy cream
- 1 teaspoon light agave syrup
- 1 teaspoon freshly squeezed lemon juice
- Pinch of salt

INSTRUCTIONS

1. In a large bowl, mash the strawberries and sugar together using a fork.

2. Add the remaining ingredients to the mashed strawberries and mix well until the sugar is completely dissolved.

3. Transfer the mixture to an empty pint, cover with the lid, and freeze for 24 hours.

4. After freezing, remove the pint from the freezer and take off the lid.

5. Select the ICE CREAM setting.

6. Once processing is complete, either add mix-ins or serve the ice cream immediately.

TIP: After processing, Add 3 tablespoons of dark chocolate chips as a MIX-IN.

VEGAN RASPBERRY ICE CREAM

PREP TIME 5 min. Freeze Time 1 d   SERVINGS 4
INGREDIENTS

- 225g fresh raspberries / 7.88oz fresh raspberries
- 3 tablespoons caster sugar
- 200ml whippable oat cream / 7fl. oz whippable oat cream
- 2 tablespoons light agave syrup
- Pinch of salt

INSTRUCTIONS

1. In a large bowl, mash the raspberries and sugar together using a fork.
2. Add the remaining ingredients to the mashed raspberries and mix well until the sugar is completely dissolved.
3. Transfer the mixture to an empty pint, cover with the lid, and freeze for 24 hours.
4. After freezing, remove the pint from the freezer and take off the lid.
5. Select the ICE CREAM setting.
6. Once processing is complete, either add mix-ins or serve the ice cream immediately.

NOTES

- If oat cream is not available, substitute it with your favorite plant-based whippable cream.
- **Tip:** After processing, Add 3 tablespoons of dark chocolate chips as a mix-in.

VEGAN BANOFFEE PIE ICE CREAM

PREP TIME 5 min. Freeze Time 1 d   SERVINGS 4

INGREDIENTS

FOR THE ICE CREAM

- 400g ripe bananas / 14oz ripe bananas
- 1 tbsp maple syrup
- OPTIONAL TOPPINGS
- 4 tbsp coconut yogurt
- 2–4 chocolate digestive biscuits, broken into small pieces

INSTRUCTION

1. Peel the bananas and roughly mash them in a large bowl using a fork. Add the maple syrup and mash again until well combined.
2. Spoon the mixture into an empty pint, cover with the storage lid, and freeze for 24 hours.
3. After freezing, remove the pint from the freezer and take off the lid.
4. Select the LITE ICE CREAM setting. If necessary, select RE-SPIN to achieve a creamier result.
5. Once processing is complete, either add mix-ins or serve the ice cream immediately.
6. Top with a spoonful of coconut yogurt and sprinkle digestive pieces over the top.

NOTES

To keep this recipe vegan, use vegan biscuits

VEGAN HONEYCOMB CRUNCH ICE CREAM

PREP TIME 5 min. Freeze Time 1 d   SERVINGS 4

INGREDIENTS

- 0.63oz / 18g vegan cream cheese
- 1.93oz / 55g caster sugar
- 8.75fl. oz / 250ml oat milk
- 4.38fl. oz / 125ml whippable oat cream
- 1 ½ teaspoons vanilla extract
- 40g honeycomb pieces or vegan chocolate-covered honeycomb pieces, for mix-in

INSTRUCTION

1. In a medium bowl, mix the cream cheese and sugar until well combined.
2. Add the milk, cream, and vanilla, and mix until the sugar is dissolved.
3. Transfer the mixture to an empty pint, cover with the lid, and freeze for 24 hours.
4. After freezing, remove the pint from the freezer and take off the lid.
5. Select the ICE CREAM setting.
6. With a spoon, create a 4 cm wide hole that reaches the bottom of the pint. Pour honeycomb pieces to the hole and process again using the MIX-IN program.

7. Once the process is completed, remove the ice cream from the pint
8. serve immediately.

NOTES

- If oat milk and cream are not available, substitute with your favorite plant-based whippable cream and milk.
- During the MIX-IN process, it's okay for the ice cream to approach or touch the MAX FILL line.

VEGAN BUTTER-PECAN ICE CREAM

PREP TIME 30 min. Freeze Time 1 d   SERVINGS 4

INGREDIENTS

- 50 grams (1.75 oz) plant-based butter or margarine
- 50 grams (1.75 oz) roughly chopped pecans, for mix-in
- 120 ml (1/2 cup) unsweetened almond milk
- 200 ml (3/4 cup + 1 tablespoon) almond cream
- 80 grams (2.8 oz) soft dark brown sugar
- 2 tablespoons (16 grams) cornflour
- Pinch of salt
- 1 teaspoon (5 ml) vanilla extract

INSTRUCTIONS

1. Over low heat melt butter in a medium saucepan. Add pecans and cook for about 3 minutes, or until the pecans turn a deep brown color and smell toasted and nutty.

2. Place a sieve over a small bowl and drain the toasted pecans thoroughly in the sieve. Reserve the melted butter and store the pecans in an airtight container if not using immediately.

3. Return the reserved butter to the saucepan and add almond milk, almond cream, sugar, cornflour, and salt. Stir over medium heat until the sugar is completely dissolved and the mixture starts to bubble.

4. Reduce the heat to low and simmer for 1–2 minutes, whisking constantly, until the mixture thickens slightly.

5. Remove the saucepan from heat and stir in the vanilla. Pour the mixture into the pint and place the pint in an ice bath. Once cooled, position the storage lid on the pint and freeze for 24 hours.

6. After freezing, remove the pint from the freezer and take off the lid.

7. Select the ICE CREAM setting.

8. With a spoon, create a 4 cm wide hole that reaches the bottom of the pint. Add the toasted pecans to the hole and process again using the MIX-IN program.

9. Once the process is completed, remove the ice cream from the pint and serve immediately.

DAIRY-FREE PUMPKIN ICE CREAM

PREP TIME 20 min. Freeze Time 1 d SERVINGS 4

INGREDIENTS

- 330g / 2 cups butternut squash, cut in 1-inch cubes
- 240ml / 1 cup unsweetened oat milk
- 180ml / 3/4 cup unsweetened coconut cream
- 2 tablespoons pumpkin pie spice
- 3 tablespoons maple syrup

INSTRUCTIONS

1. In a small saucepan over medium-high heat, Place all ingredients and whisk until fully combined. Cook until the butternut squash is fork-tender, about 10 to 15 minutes.
2. Remove the base from heat and transfer to a blender pitcher. Blend until smooth, about 60 seconds.
3. Pour the base through a fine-mesh strainer into an empty CREAMi Pint. Place the pint into an ice bath. After cooling, place the storage lid on the pint and freeze for 24 hours.
4. After freezing, remove the pint from the freezer and take off the lid.
5. Select the ICE CREAM setting.
6. Once the process is completed, remove the ice cream from the pint
7. serve immediately.

VEGAN BURNT SUGAR ICE CREAM

PREP TIME 15 min. Freeze Time 1 d   SERVINGS 4

INGREDIENTS

- 3 vegan eggs
- 240ml / 1 cup unsweetened soy milk
- 120ml / 1/2 cup unsweetened vegan creamer
- 50g / 1/4 cup packed dark brown sugar, plus more for garnish
- Pinch of kosher salt
- 50g / 1/4 cup granulated sugar
- 1 tablespoon water

INSTRUCTIONS

1. Prepare vegan eggs as instructed on the box.
2. In a medium bowl, add the soy milk, creamer, brown sugar, salt, and prepared vegan egg. Whisk until fully combined.
3. In a medium saucepan over medium heat, place the granulated sugar and water. Cook, swirling occasionally, about 5 minutes until the mixture begins to caramelize.
4. Once the sugar has caramelized, then slowly add in the vegan egg mixture and gently stir to combine.
5. Remove the base from heat and pour it into an empty CREAMi Pint. Place the pint in an ice bath. After cooling, place the storage lid on the pint and freeze for 24 hours.
6. After freezing, remove the pint from the freezer and take off the lid.
7. Select the ICE CREAM setting.

8. When processing is complete, remove the ice cream from the pint, top with brown sugar, and serve immediately.

VEGAN MANGO COCONUT ICE CREAM

PREP TIME 10 min. Freeze Time 1 d   SERVINGS 3

Calories 200

INGREDIENTS

- 300 grams (10.6 oz) mango, peeled and diced
- 200 ml (3/4 cup + 1 tablespoon) coconut milk
- 50 grams (1.75 oz) coconut sugar or sweetening agent of your choice (brown sugar, agave syrup, maple syrup, sweetener)
- 1 tablespoon (15 ml) lemon juice

INSTRUCTIONS

1. Combine the diced mango, coconut milk, coconut sugar, and lemon juice, in a blender. Blend until smooth.
2. Pour the mixture into the Ninja Creami deluxe container and freeze for 24 hours.
3. After freezing, use the Lite Ice Cream setting.

4. At the end of the cycle, add two shots of the liquid of your choice and restart a re-spin again for an even smoother texture.

TIP

For an irresistible adult variation, add two shots of rum at the end.

VEGAN BANANA MAPLE PECAN ICE CREAM

PREP TIME 10 min. Freeze Time 1 d   SERVINGS 4

INGREDIENTS

- 14oz / 400g ripe bananas, peeled
- 2.63oz / 75g maple syrup, plus extra to serve
- 2.63oz / 75g pecan halves, for mix-in

INSTRUCTIONS

1. In a large bowl, mash the bananas well, then spoon them into the pint. Stir in the maple syrup, cover with the storage lid, and freeze for 24 hours.
2. While the base is freezing, preheat the oven to 180°C. Spread the pecans on a lined baking tray and bake for 6 minutes, or until lightly toasted. Allow them to cool and store in an airtight container if not using immediately.

3. After freezing, remove the pint from the freezer and take off the lid.
4. Select the ICE CREAM setting.
5. Create a 4 cm wide hole that reaches the bottom of the pint, using a spoon. Add pecan halves to the hole (save four for serving) and process using the MIX-IN program.
6. Once the process is completed, remove the ice cream from the pint
7. Serve immediately, placing a pecan half on each serving.

DAIRY-FREE VANILLA COCONUT ICE CREAM

PREP TIME 5 min. Freeze Time 1 d SERVINGS 4

INGREDIENTS
- 1 can (400g) full-fat unsweetened coconut milk
- 3.33oz / 95g caster sugar
- 1 tsp vanilla extract

INSTRUCTIONS
1. Stir or Shake the can of coconut milk.
2. In a medium bowl, whisk all ingredients together until

well combined and the sugar is dissolved.

3. Pour the mixture into an empty pint, cover with the lid, and freeze for 24 hours.
4. After freezing, remove the pint from the freezer and take off the lid.
5. Select the ICE CREAM setting.
6. Once processing is complete, either add mix-ins or serve the ice cream immediately.

TIP

- Create new flavors by adding 2 tablespoons of cocoa powder for chocolate coconut ice cream, 2 tablespoons of instant coffee for coffee coconut ice cream, or substituting vanilla extract with lemon extract for lemon coconut ice cream.

GLUTEN-FREE & VEGAN MINCE PIE ICE CREAM

PREP TIME 7 min. Freeze Time 1 d   SERVINGS 4

INGREDIENTS

FOR THE ICE CREAM

- 0.88oz / 25g vegan butter
- 4.2fl. oz / 120ml unsweetened nut milk
- 7fl. oz / 200ml plant-based single cream
- 2.8oz / 80g raw cane sugar or coconut sugar
- 1/2 Zest unwaxed orange

- 1/2 Zest unwaxed lemon
- 2 tbsp cornflour
- 1 tsp vanilla paste
- 1 tsp ground mixed spice
- Pinch of salt

FOR THE MIX-IN
- 60g/2 mini gluten-free vegan mince pies (quartered)

INSTRUCTIONS

1. Add all the ice cream ingredients to a medium-sized non-stick pan.
2. Place the pan over medium heat until the sugar completely dissolves and the mixture begins to bubble.
3. Reduce the heat to low and simmer for 1–2 minutes, whisking constantly, until the mixture thickens slightly.
4. Remove the saucepan from heat and pour the mixture into the pint. Place a layer of clingfilm over the mixture and gently smooth it to prevent a skin from forming on top.
5. Place the pint in an ice bath to cool completely. Once cooled, cover with the storage lid and freeze for 24 hours.
6. After freezing, remove the pint from the freezer and take off the lid.
7. Select the ICE CREAM setting.
8. Once the process finishes, create a 4 cm wide hole that reaches the bottom of the pint using a spoon. Add the quartered mini mince pies to the hole and process again using the MIX-IN function.
9. Once the process is completed, remove the ice cream and serve immediately

DAIRY-FREE MINT CHIP ICE CREAM

PREP TIME 5 min. Freeze Time 1 d   SERVINGS 4

INGREDIENTS

- 1 can (400g) full-fat unsweetened coconut milk
- 95g / 3.33oz caster sugar
- 1/2 tsp peppermint extract
- 45g / 1.58oz vegan mini chocolate chips, for mix-in

INSTRUCTIONS

1. Stir or shake the can of coconut milk.
2. whisk together the coconut milk, sugar, and peppermint extract in a medium bowl until well combined and the sugar is dissolved.
3. Pour the mixture into an empty pint, cover with the lid, and freeze for 24 hours.
4. After freezing, remove the pint from the freezer and take off the lid.
5. Select the ICE CREAM setting.
6. Once the process finishes, create a 4 cm wide hole that reaches the bottom of the pint using a spoon. Add 45g of vegan mini chocolate chips to the hole and then process again using the MIX-IN program.
7. It's fine if the level is above the MAX FILL line.
8. Once the process is completed, remove the ice cream from the pint and serve immediately.

DAIRY-FREE APPLE STRUDEL ICE CREAM

PREP TIME 10 min. Freeze Time 1 d   SERVINGS 4

INGREDIENTS

- 1 large apple, peeled and cut into small dices
- 250g / 8.75oz oat cream (8.3% fat)
- 60ml / 2.1fl. oz almond milk
- 50g / 1.75oz brown sugar
- 1 tsp ground cinnamon
- 30g / 1.05oz coconut oil
- 1/2 Juice from lemon

INSTRUCTIONS

1. Combine all ingredients in a medium saucepan, stirring until well mixed.
2. Set the saucepan over medium heat and stir continuously with a wooden spoon until the sugar dissolves completely.
3. Take the saucepan off the heat and transfer the ice cream base to a pint container.
4. Place the container in an ice bath. Once cooled, cover the container with a storage lid and freeze for 24 hours.
5. After freezing, take the pint out of the freezer and remove the lid.
6. Select the "ICE CREAM" setting.
7. Once the process is finished, scoop out the ice cream from the pint and serve right away.

VEGAN VANILLA ICE CREAM

PREP TIME 5 min. Freeze Time 1 d   SERVINGS 4

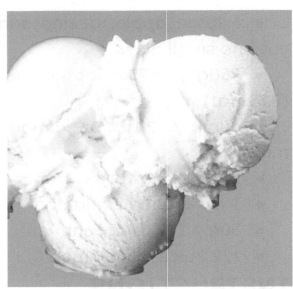

INGREDIENTS

- 18g / 0.63oz vegan cream cheese
- 55g / 1.93oz caster sugar
- 250ml / 8.75fl. oz oat milk
- 125ml / 4.38fl. oz whippable oat cream
- 1 1/2 tsp vanilla extract

INSTRUCTIONS

1. Combine cream cheese and sugar in a medium bowl until thoroughly mixed.
2. Add the remaining ingredients and continue mixing until the sugar is fully dissolved.
3. Pour the mixture into an empty pint container, cover with a lid, and freeze for 24 hours.
4. After freezing, take the pint out of the freezer and remove the lid.
5. Select the "ICE CREAM" setting.
6. Once the processing is done, you can add mix-ins or scoop the ice cream from the pint and serve immediately.

TIP: For added flavor, MIX-IN 3 tablespoons of dark chocolate chips after processing.

VEGAN CHOCOLATE ICE CREAM

PREP TIME 10 min. Freeze Time 1 d   SERVINGS 3

INGREDIENTS

- 1 cup (240 grams) silken tofu
- 3 tablespoons (15 grams) cocoa powder or to taste (if you really like cocoa, use 1/4 cup (20 grams))
- 1/4 cup (50 grams) brown sugar (or white)
- 1 teaspoon (5 ml) vanilla
- 1 cup (240 ml) almond milk
- pinch salt
- stevia o taste

INSTRUCTIONS

1. Puree all ingredients in a high-speed blender until very creamy and smooth.
2. Transfer the mixture into the Creami pint and freeze for at least 24 hours.
3. Once completely frozen, process in the Creami machine.
4. Select ICE cream
5. Scoop and enjoy!

VEGAN CHOCOLATE PEANUT BUTTER CUP

PREP TIME 10 min. Freeze Time 1 d   SERVINGS 4

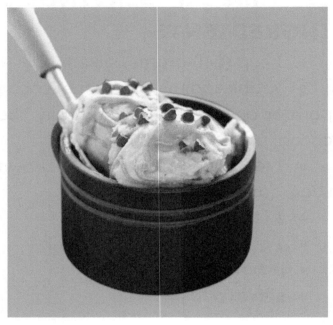

INGREDIENTS

- 1 cup / 133 grams of cooked white sweet potato (Hannah Yam)
- 1 1/4 cup / 296 ml of chocolate almond milk (plain plant-milk will work fine in a pinch)
- 6 Medjool dates, pitted
- 2 tablespoons (16 grams) oat flour
- 1/4 teaspoon (1 gram) vanilla powder or 1 teaspoon (5 ml) pure vanilla extract
- 2 tablespoons (10 grams) cacao powder
- 1/4 teaspoon (1.5 grams) salt (optional)
- 1/4 to 1/2 teaspoon (0.5 to 1 gram) guar gum (can probably go without if you don't have it, it's a thickener; start with 1/4 teaspoon, you can add more if necessary)
- 1 tablespoon (8 grams) peanut butter powder (I use Naked PB, it doesn't contain salt or sugar)

INGREDIENTS

1. Blend all ingredients EXCEPT peanut butter powder in a high-speed blender, placing the liquid at the bottom for optimal blending.

2. Transfer the mixture to the CREAMi container, ensuring the top is flattened for even freezing.
3. Freeze for 24 hours, then run the mixture through the CREAMi machine on the lite ice cream setting. A second run may be needed, but it's unlikely.
4. Create a well in the center of the ice cream and place the peanut butter powder in the center.
5. Run the machine on the mix-in setting.

NOTES

- You might have a little extra mixture due to the "fill line" on the ice cream container. Save the extra in the fridge to eat as pudding or refreeze after enjoying some prepared ice cream.

PEANUT BUTTER VEGAN BANANA CHOCOLATE CHIP ICE CREAM

PREP TIME 10 min. Freeze Time 1 d   SERVINGS 4

INGREDIENTS

- 4 to 5 very ripe fresh bananas, peeled
- 1/4 teaspoon (1 gram) vanilla powder or 1/4 teaspoon (1.25 ml) vanilla extract
- 1/4 cup (30 grams) peanut butter powder (PB2 Pure, no salt or sugar) or 1/4 cup (65 grams) peanut butter

- Unsweetened plant milk as needed
- 1/4 cup (45 grams) unsweetened chocolate chips

INSTRUCTIONS

1. Break bananas into the CREAMi pint container and mash them with a fork.
2. Add the peanut butter powder or your preferred nut butter and the vanilla powder or vanilla extract. Stir well to combine.
3. Add the peanut butter powder or your preferred nut butter and the vanilla powder or vanilla extract. Stir well to combine.
4. If the mixture does not reach the maximum fill line, add additional banana or a bit of plant milk and mix thoroughly. Even out the top of the mixture to make it level.
5. Put the lid on the container, and place it in the freezer for 24 hours, ensuring the pint container is level so the mixture will freeze evenly.
6. After 24 hours, take the pint out of the freezer and let it rest on the counter for 5-10 minutes.
7. Select the lite ice cream setting. If the mixture appears powdery, put it back in the Ninja appliance and use the re-spin setting.
8. To add chocolate chips, make a 1 1/2" wide well in the center of the ice cream using a spoon, all the way to the bottom, and pour in about 1/4 cup of chocolate chips.
9. Place the CREAMi pint back on the appliance and use the Mix-In setting to incorporate the chocolate chips throughout the ice cream.
10. Scoop and enjoy!

Leftover Storage

- If you have at least 1/3 of a pint of leftover ice cream, smooth out the top so it is level.
- Put the lid on and place it back in the freezer.

- When ready to serve again, spin it, and it will be like freshly made ice cream! Enjoy!

NOTES

Substitutions:

Bananas: Try oven-roasted Japanese sweet potatoes or Hannah yams, peeled and mashed.

Peanut Butter Powder: Use natural peanut butter or your choice of nut butter.

Cacao Chips (unsweetened): Use your choice of chocolate chips or cacao nibs.

Peanut Butter: Leave out the peanut butter or peanut butter powder to make banana chocolate chip ice cream.

COCONUT CREAMI ICE CREAM

PREP TIME 5 min. Freeze Time 1 d   SERVINGS 3

INGREDIENTS

- 1 can of coconut cream
- Coconut shavings
- Agave syrup
- 2 shots of vegetable milk

INSTRUCTIONS

1. Open the can of coconut cream and pour its contents into the Creami deluxe Pint.
2. Add a generous handful of coconut shavings. Stir in the agave syrup to your desired level of sweetness.
3. Close the lid of the Creami deluxe and place the mixture in the freezer for 24 hours.
4. Select the Ice Cream option to mix
5. Once the cycle is complete, open the lid, add the 2 shots of vegetable milk, and run a re-spin cycle until the texture is creamy.

VEGAN SALTED CARAMEL ICE CREAM

PREP TIME 5 min. Freeze Time 1 d   SERVINGS 1

INGREDIENTS

- 1 cup (240 grams) cooked yellow sweet potato flesh (Hannah sweet potato)
- 1 cup (240 ml) non-dairy milk
- 1/2 cup (100 grams) coconut sugar
- 1-2 tablespoons (15-30 grams) macadamia nut butter or raw cashew butter (optional)

- 2 teaspoons (10 ml) pure vanilla extract or 1/2 teaspoon (1 gram) vanilla bean powder
- 1/2 teaspoon (2.5 grams) sea salt (a little scant)

INSTRUCTIONS

1. Puree all ingredients in a high-speed blender, until very smooth.
2. Transfer the mixture to a CREAMi deluxe Pint and place it in the freezer for 24 hours.
3. Once fully frozen, place the container in the CREAMi machine and set to the ice cream function, running through that cycle twice.
4. Once the mixture reaches an easily scoopable, smooth texture, serve!

NOTES

- **Coconut Sugar Note:** Coconut sugar has a natural caramel flavor, making it perfect for this recipe. Do not substitute regular unrefined sugar. Date sugar can be used as a substitute, but it will result in a different flavor and texture. I find that 1/2 cup of coconut sugar yields a mixture that is sweet enough. If you prefer it sweeter or with a stronger caramel flavor, you can add another 1-2 tablespoons of sugar to taste. While you can substitute pitted dates for about half of the sugar (using 1/3 cup of pitted dates and 1/4 cup of coconut sugar), the flavor is not as good as when using coconut sugar alone.

VEGAN PISTACHIO ICE CREAM

PREP TIME 15 min. Freeze Time 1 d   SERVINGS 4

INGREDIENTS

- 180ml / 3/4 cup cashew milk
- 240ml / 1 cup coconut milk
- 67g / 1/3 cup sugar
- 2 tablespoons maple syrup
- 2 tablespoons vegan cream cheese
- 1/4 teaspoon almond extract
- 1/8 teaspoon salt
- 1 drop green food coloring, optional
- 37.5g / 1/4 cup pistachios, shelled, coarsely chopped, plus more for garnish

INSTRUCTIONS

1. Add cashew milk, coconut milk, sugar, maple syrup, and cream cheese in a medium saucepan. Whisk until the mixture is smooth and dissolved.
2. Place the saucepan on the stove over medium heat and cook for 5-7 minutes.
3. Add almond extract, salt, and food coloring (if preferred). Stir to combine.
4. Remove the mixture from heat and pour it into an empty CREAMi Pint up to the MAX FILL line.
5. Place the pint into an ice bath to cool. Once cooled, cover with the storage lid and freeze for 24 hours.
6. After 24 hours, select the ICE CREAM function on the CREAMi machine.

7. Using a spoon, create a 1 1/2-inch wide hole that reaches the bottom of the pint. Add pistachios to the hole and process again using the MIX-IN program.

8. Once processing is complete, remove from the pint and serve immediately.

CREAMSICLE VEGAN PROTEIN ICE CREAM

PREP TIME 15 min. Freeze Time 1 d   SERVINGS 4

INGREDIENTS

- 2 packed cups (300 grams) orange segments (make sure seeds and peel are removed)
- 1 cup (240 ml) non-dairy milk of choice
- 1/2 cup (120 grams) mashed ripe banana
- 1/2 cup (120 grams) silken tofu or okara
- 2 scoops (about 60 grams) vanilla or plain protein powder
- 2 teaspoons (10 ml) vanilla extract or 1/2 teaspoon (1 gram) vanilla powder

INSTRUCTIONS

1. Blend all the ingredients until smooth.

2. Pour the blended mixture into a Creami deluxe pint.
3. Freeze the mixture for 24 hours.
4. After freezing, spin on the lite ice cream setting.
5. If the texture is still powdery, use the respin function and add a few tablespoons of non-dairy milk if needed.
6. Once the desired consistency is reached, serve immediately.

Nutrition Information: <u>SERVING SIZE: 1</u>

Calories: 158kcal   Carbohydrates: 19g   Protein: 16g   Fat: 3g

VEGAN BANANA SPLIT ICE CREAM

PREP TIME 15 min. Freeze Time 1 d   SERVINGS 4

INGREDIENTS

- 1 ½ cups (360 grams) mashed ripe bananas or white sweet potato puree
- 1 ½ cups (225 grams) mashed strawberries
- ½ cup (120 grams) crushed pineapple and juice
- ½ cup (120 ml) non-dairy milk as needed, to fill the container to the max line
- 2 tablespoons (10-15 grams) cocoa or cacao powder to taste – you might need less
- 1 teaspoon (5 ml) vanilla extract

- Sweetener to taste (optional; use only if necessary, can use whole dates, date paste, or maple syrup)

INSTRUCTIONS

1. Start by mashing the bananas and strawberries together in the Creami deluxe pint.
2. Add in the crushed pineapple (including its juice), cocoa powder, and vanilla extract.
3. Alternatively, you can blend the mixture in a small blender.
4. Taste the mixture and add sweetener if needed. Sometimes the fruits are sweet enough by themselves!
5. Freeze the mixture for 24 hours
6. Once frozen, spin the mixture on the lite ice cream setting of your Creami deluxe.
7. If the texture remains powdery, add a few tablespoons of non-dairy milk and respin.
8. Once the desired consistency is reached, serve immediately.

Nutrition Information: SERVING SIZE: 1
Calories: 132kcal   Carbohydrates: 31g   Protein: 3g

Fat: 1g   Fiber: 5g   Sugar: 18g

VEGAN LONDON FOG ICE CREAM

PREP TIME 10 min. Freeze Time 1 d   SERVINGS 3

INGREDIENTS

- 3 cups (720 ml) hot water
- 3 teaspoons (6 grams) loose leaf Earl Grey tea – regular or decaf, or 6 teabags
- 3 tablespoons (45 grams) cashew butter OR 3 tablespoons (24 grams) JOI oat milk powder, or 1 cup (80 grams) oats (you can strain or not)
- 4.5 dates OR liquid sweetener of choice to taste (like maple syrup, date syrup, or simple syrup, etc.)
- 1½ teaspoons (7.5 ml) vanilla extract OR 1 teaspoon (2 grams) vanilla powder

INSTRUCTIONS

1. Steep the tea for 5 minutes in hot water before straining into a blender. Let it cool.
2. Blend the cooled tea with all the other ingredients.
3. Note: If you use whole rolled oats, you can choose to strain the mixture or leave it as is.
4. Pour the mixture into a Creami deluxe pint.
5. Mix in the vanilla extract.
6. To fill to the max line, add water or nondairy milk.
7. Taste and adjust the sweetener if needed.
8. Freeze the mixture for 24 hours.
9. After freezing, spin the mixture on the ice cream setting.
10.   If the texture is still powdery, use the respin button.

11. Once the desired consistency is reached, serve immediately.

Nutrition Information: SERVING SIZE: 1

Calories: 132kcal   Carbohydrates: 12g   Protein: 3g   Fat: 8g
Fiber: 1g   Sugar: 7g

VEGAN CANTALOUPE ICE CREAM

PREP TIME 10 min. Freeze Time 1 d   SERVINGS 3

INGREDIENTS

- 1 ½ cups (360 grams) mashed fresh cantaloupe
- 1 ¼ cups (300 ml) non-dairy milk, or more if needed to reach the max fill line
- 3 tablespoons (45 ml) vegan honey to taste, or other liquid sweetener – even date paste
- 1 teaspoon (5 ml) vanilla extract

INSTRUCTIONS

1. Blend all the ingredients together until smooth. If needed, Taste and adjust the sweetener.
2. Pour the mixture into a Creami deluxe pint.
3. Freeze for 24 hours.
4. Level off the pint if there is a hump or volcano shape.
5. Spin on the lite ice cream setting.
6. If the texture is not creamy, spin again using the respin function.

7. If it is still not smooth, add 2 tablespoons of water and respin again.

8. Once the desired consistency is reached, serve immediately.

Nutrition Information: SERVING SIZE: 1

Calories: 127kcal   Carbohydrates: 23g   Protein: 3g

Fat: 2g   Fiber: 1g   Sugar: 21g

VEGAN CHERRY ICE CREAM

PREP TIME 15 min. Freeze Time 1 d   SERVINGS 3

INGREDIENTS

- 1 ½ cups (360 ml) non-dairy milk
- 3 cups (450 grams) pitted cherries
- 1 ½ tablespoons (22.5 ml) maple syrup or sweetener of choice to taste
- 1.5 teaspoons (7.5 ml) vanilla extract
- Optional Mix-in:
- 5. ¼ cup + 2 tablespoons (60 grams) vegan chocolate chips or chopped chocolate bar

INSTRUCTIONS

1. Add 1 cup of milk, vanilla, and 1 tablespoon of maple syrup to a Ninja Creami deluxe pint and whisk together well.

2. Put the cherries in and mash them with a potato masher to break them up slightly. Taste and add extra sweetener if the cherries aren't very sweet.

3. Ensure the cherries are submerged in the liquid. Add more milk or mashed cherries to reach the fill line if needed.
4. Freeze the mixture for 24 hours.
5. If your freezer is extra cold, let the pint sit out for 10-15 minutes or run the outside under warm water to soften.
6. Scrape the top flat with a spoon if there is a hump or volcano.
7. Spin on the lite ice cream setting.
8. If the mixture is crumbly, add 1 tablespoon of liquid and spin on the respin setting.
9. Make a tunnel in the ice cream and add in the chocolate, then use the mix-in button.
10.   You may need to mix the ice cream a little more to distribute the chocolate evenly.
11. Enjoy!

VEGAN OATMEAL RAISIN COOKIE ICE CREAM

PREP TIME 5 min. Freeze Time 1 d   SERVINGS 3

INGREDIENTS

- 240ml / 1 cup oat milk
- 110g / 1/2 cup brown sugar
- 1/4 teaspoon cinnamon
- 2 tablespoons vegan cream cheese
- 25g / 1/4 cup oatmeal raisin cookies, crumbled

INSTRUCTIONS

1. Add oat milk, brown sugar, cinnamon, and vegan cream cheese in a blender. Blend on high until smooth.
2. Pour the base into an empty CREAMi Pint. Put the storage lid on the pint and freeze for 24 hours.
3. After freezing, remove the pint from the freezer and take off the lid.
4. Select the ICE CREAM function on the CREAMi machine.
5. create a 1 1/2-inch wide hole that reaches the bottom of the pint using a spoon. Add 1/2 cup of crumbled oatmeal raisin cookies to the hole.
6. Process again using the MIX-IN program.
7. Once the process is completed, remove the ice cream from the pint and serve immediately.

VEGAN PINEAPPLE DOLE WHIP

PREP TIME 5 min. Freeze Time 1 d   SERVINGS 3

INGREDIENTS

- 4 cups (600 grams) pineapple in juice, canned or fresh
- ½ cup (120 ml) non-dairy milk, as needed after first blend

INSTRUCTIONS

1. Blend the pineapple and its juice in a blender, or dump the pineapple chunks or crushed pineapple directly into a Creami pint.
2. Ensure the mixture does not go over the max fill line. Smooth the top so it's even, and place the pint on a level spot in the freezer. Freeze for 24 hours.

3. Turn on the Creami machine and select the sorbet setting.

4. If the mixture is crumbly, add a few tablespoons of nondairy milk and use the respin button.

5. Depending on how cold your freezer is, you may need to respin again.

NOTES

- Feel free to add some vanilla extract or a teaspoon of real rum for extra flavor.

- If your can of pineapple in juice doesn't fill up the pint, add nondairy milk to reach the max fill line.

Nutrition Information: SERVING SIZE: 1

Calories: 122kcal   Carbohydrates: 29g   Protein: 2g   Fat: 1g
Fiber: 2g   Sugar: 27g

UNREAL VEGAN ICE CREAM SUNDAE

PREP TIME 5 min. Freeze Time 1 d   SERVINGS 4

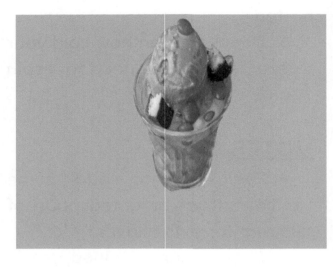

INGREDIENTS

- 100 grams (1/2 cup) granulated sugar
- 1 teaspoon (2 grams) blue spirulina powder
- 1/4 teaspoon (1.5 grams) kosher salt
- 1 can (14 oz / 400 ml) full-fat unsweetened coconut milk
- 1 teaspoon (5 ml) vanilla extract
- 2 tablespoons (30 grams) UNREAL dark chocolate crispy quinoa gems OR dark chocolate peanut gems, plus additional for garnish
- 2 each dark chocolate coconut bars, broken into 1/2" pieces
- 4 each dark chocolate peanut butter cups, each cut in half

INSTRUCTIONS

1. Whisk together sugar, spirulina powder, and kosher salt in a medium-sized bowl.
2. Slowly pour in the coconut milk while whisking to combine.
3. Add in the vanilla and stir until all ingredients are incorporated and the sugar is dissolved.
4. Pour the base into an empty CREAMi deluxe pint. Put the storage lid on the pint and freeze for 24 hours.
5. After freezing, select the ICE CREAM function on the CREAMi machine.

6. Create a 1 ½-inch wide hole that reaches the bottom of the pint using a spoon. During this step, it is OK for your treat to press over the MAX FILL line.
7. Add the 2 tablespoons of gems and dark chocolate coconut bar pieces to the hole, and process again using the MIX-IN program.
8. Once processing is complete, scoop the ice cream into desired cups and decorate with peanut butter cups and more UNREAL gems.
9. Serve immediately.

DAIRY-FREE COFFEE ICE CREAM

PREP TIME 5 min. Freeze Time 1 d SERVINGS 4

INGREDIENTS

- 256g / 1 cup + 2 tablespoons unsweetened coconut cream
- 150g / 3/4 cup granulated sugar
- 2 tablespoons instant coffee
- 370g / 1 1/2 cups rice milk
- 1 1/2 teaspoons vanilla extract

INSTRUCTIONS

1. Whisk the unsweetened coconut cream until smooth in a large bowl.

2. Add the remaining ingredients to the bowl and whisk until well combined and the sugar is dissolved.
3. Pour the base into an empty CREAMi Deluxe Pint. Put the storage lid on the pint and freeze for 24 hours.
4. After freezing, remove the Deluxe Pint from the freezer and take off the lid.
5. Select (TOP, FULL, or BOTTOM) then select ICE CREAM.
6. Once processing is complete, if desired, add mix-ins, or remove the ice cream from the Deluxe Pint and serve immediately.

VEGAN LIME FROZEN YOGURT

PREP TIME 5 min. Freeze Time 1 d   SERVINGS 4

INGREDIENTS

- 2 limes (juice and zest)
- 1 ½ cups (360 grams) plant-based yogurt
- ¾ cup (150 grams) sugar
- ¼ cup (60 ml) plant-based milk
- 1 teaspoon (5 ml) vanilla extract
- tiny pinch salt
- lime
- maple syrup

INSTRUCTIONS

1. Juice and zest two limes. Set the zest aside.
2. Blend everything except the lime zest in a high-speed blender until very smooth. Then stir in the lime zest.

3. Pour the yogurt mixture into the Creami deluxe container and freeze for 24 hours.
4. Allow the mixture to defrost for about 5 minutes, then process in the Creami deluxe using the ice cream setting. Use the respin function if it's not smooth enough.
5. Sprinkle additional lime zest on top if desired, and drizzle with a bit of maple syrup and lime juice.
6. Serve and enjoy!

Nutrition Information: SERVING SIZE: 1
CALORIES: 238 TOTAL FAT: 2g FIBER: 1g SUGAR: 48g PROTEIN: 5g

BLUEBERRY–LEMON VEGAN FROZEN YOGURT

PREP TIME 5 min. Freeze Time 1 d   SERVINGS 4

INGREDIENTS
- 125g fresh blueberries / 4.38oz fresh blueberries
- 60g caster sugar / 2.1oz caster sugar
- 180g plain, unsweetened Greek-style plant-based yogurt / 6.3oz plain, unsweetened Greek-style plant-based yogurt

- 125ml whippable oat cream / 4.38fl. oz whippable oat cream
- 1 tablespoon light agave syrup
- 1 teaspoon vanilla extract
- 1/2 teaspoon lemon zest
- Pinch of salt

INSTRUCTIONS

1. Gently mash the blueberries and caster sugar together in a medium bowl using a fork.
2. Add the remaining ingredients and mix until fully combined and the sugar is dissolved.
3. Transfer the mixture to an empty pint, cover with the lid, and freeze for at least 24 hours.
4. After freezing, remove the pint from the freezer and take off the lid.
5. Select the ICE CREAM setting.
6. Once processing is complete, either add mix-ins or serve the ice cream immediately.

NOTES

Oat cream can be swapped for your favorite plant-based whippable cream.

- If your freezer is set to a very cold temperature, the ice cream may appear crumbly. If this happens, select RE-SPIN to process the mixture a little more.

VEGAN MEYER LEMON THYME SORBET

PREP TIME 30 min. Freeze Time 1 d   SERVINGS 4

INGREDIENTS

- 1 tablespoon invert sugar or corn syrup
- 237ml / 1 cup water
- 100g / 1/2 cup white sugar
- 6 sprigs thyme
- 178ml / 3/4 cup meyer lemon juice
- zest of 2 lemons
- pinch of salt

INSTRUCTIONS

1. In a medium saucepan, add syrup, water, sugar, and thyme. Whisk to combine.
2. Place the saucepan on the stove over medium heat and bring to a simmer.
3. Remove the thyme sprigs.
4. Whisk in lemon juice, lemon zest, and salt.
5. Remove the base from heat and pour it into an empty CREAMi Pint. Place the pint into an ice bath to cool.
6. Once cooled, put the storage lid on the pint and freeze for 24 hours.
7. After freezing, remove the pint from the freezer and take off the lid.
8. Select SORBET.
9. When processing is complete, remove the sorbet from the pint and serve immediately.

TIP

- If your freezer is set to a very cold temperature, the sorbet may appears crumbly. If this happens, run the RE-SPIN program to process the mixture a little more if not adding mix-ins.

VEGAN MANGONADA SORBET

PREP TIME 10 min. Freeze Time 1 d   SERVINGS 4
INGREDIENTS

- 4 / 660g cups chopped mangoes
- 1/2 / 118.5ml cup water
- 1/4 / 59ml cup lime juice
- 1/3–1/2 (67g -100g) cup sugar
- 2 tablespoons chamoy
- Tajin, as desired

INSTRUCTIONS

1. In a blender, puree the mangoes and water on high speed. Transfer the mixture through a fine-mesh strainer.

2. In a large bowl, combine the mango base with lime juice, sugar, and chamoy, whisking until well mixed.

3. Transfer the mixture to an empty CREAMi Deluxe Pint, cover with a storage lid, and freeze for 24 hours.

4. After freezing, remove the pint from the freezer and take off the lid.

5. Select the SORBET setting on the machine.

6. Once the processing is complete, serve the sorbet in a dish with chamoy and Tajín sprinkled on the rim. Add additional Tajín on top of the sorbet.

VEGAN STRAWBERRY SORBET

PREP TIME 5 min. Freeze Time 1 d   SERVINGS 1

INGREDIENTS

- 3 cups (450 grams) fresh sliced/roughly chopped strawberries
- 1 1/2 – 2 tablespoons (15–20 grams) white chia seeds
- 1/4 cup (60 ml) orange juice or 2 tablespoons (30 ml) water and 2 tablespoons (30 ml) pure maple syrup
- 1/2 – 1 tablespoon (7.5–15 ml) pure maple syrup (optional)
- 1/4 teaspoon (1 gram) vanilla bean powder (optional)
- Pinch of salt (optional)
- 1/2 tablespoon (4 grams) dragonfruit powder (optional)

INSTRUCTIONS

1. For the strawberries, don't worry about precision in chopping. Simply slice or cut them in half for a rough measure.
2. In a blender, add just 1 cup of the strawberries, chia seeds (1 1/2 - 2 tbsp), orange juice or water/maple syrup, and vanilla/salt/dragonfruit powder (if using). Puree until smooth.
3. Add the remaining strawberries and pulse to roughly chop, keeping some chunky consistency. Alternatively, you can dice by hand and stir into the pureed mixture, maintaining some chunks of the berries.
4. Transfer the mixture to a CREAMi deluxe pint. place it in the freezer for 24 hours.
5. Once fully frozen, remove and place in the CREAMi spin vessel.
6. Set the function to "sorbet" and let it spin at least twice.
7. Check consistency. If it's still icy or not soft enough, spin again. Once smooth and spoonable, it's ready to serve!

NOTES

- **Orange Juice Note:** If you prefer not to add a sweetener like maple syrup or date syrup, try 1/4 cup of fresh orange juice. Depending on the sweetness of the juice and the ripeness of the berries, you may still opt for a touch of maple syrup. Keep in mind that a frozen treat will taste less sweet than the room temperature mixture

PREP TIME 5 min. Freeze Time 1 d   SERVINGS 4
INGREDIENTS

- 11oz / 335g diced ripe avocado (about 3 ripe avocados)
- 5fl. oz / 150ml / unsweetened favourite plant-based milk
- 2.8oz / 80g caster sugar
- 2 tbsp freshly squeezed lime juice
- 1 tbsp light agave syrup
- 1 1/2 tsp lime zest
- Pinch of salt
- 1.4oz / 40g digestive biscuits, broken into large pieces, for mix-in

INSTRUCTIONS

1. mash the avocado with a fork in a large bowl.
2. Add the remaining ingredients (except for the biscuits) and stir well until fully combined and the sugar is dissolved.
3. Transfer the mixture to an empty pint, cover with the lid, and freeze for 24 hours.
4. After freezing, remove the pint from the freezer and take off the lid.
5. Select the GELATO setting.
6. Once the process finishes, create a 4 cm wide hole that reaches the bottom of the pint using a spoon. Add the graham cracker pieces to the hole and then process again using the MIX-IN program.
7. Once the process is completed, remove the ice cream from the pint and serve immediately.

NOTES

- During the MIX-IN process, it's okay for the ice cream to approach or touch the MAX FILL line.

CHOCOLATE THICKSHAKE

PREP TIME 16 min. Freeze Time 1 d SERVINGS 4

INGREDIENTS

- 1 x 475ml pint high quality chocolate ice cream
- 125ml / 4fl. oz barista style oat milk
- 2 tsp cocoa powder

TOPPING SUGGESTIONS (OPTIONAL)

- Whipped cream
- Sprinkles
- Maraschino/cocktail cherries
- Chocolate sauce
- Chopped nuts

INSTRUCTIONS

1. Allow the ice cream to soften enough to be easily removed from the pint and place it into the empty ice cream pint provided with the unit. If the ice cream exceeds the max line, slice off the excess, cut it into slices, and place them around the sides of the pint.

2. Add the oat milk and cocoa powder. Cover the pint with the lid and freeze for 15 minutes. Optionally, you can chill your serving glass(es) in the freezer as well.

3. After 15 minutes, take the pint out of the freezer and remove the lid. Select the "MILKSHAKE" setting.

4. Once the processing is complete, pour the milkshake into glasses and serve immediately.

5. This recipe yields enough for one large glass or two medium glasses. Top with any optional toppings and enjoy.

NOTES

- For a healthier option, use low-sugar ice cream brands such as Halo Top or Oppo. Chocolate hazelnut flavor also tastes delicious!

CONVERSION MEASUREMENT

Volume Measurements:

1 teaspoon (tsp) = 5 milliliters (ml)

1 tablespoon (tbsp) = 15 milliliters (ml)

1 fluid ounce (fl oz) = 30 milliliters (ml)

1 cup (c) = 240 milliliters (ml)

1 pint (pt) = 480 milliliters (ml)

1 quart (qt) = 960 milliliters (ml)

1 gallon (gal) = 3.8 liters (L)

Weight Measurements:

1 ounce (oz) = 28 grams (g)

1 pound (lb) = 16 ounces (oz) = 454 grams (g)

Common Ingredient Conversions:

1 stick of butter = 1/2 cup = 113 grams

1 c of all-purpose flour = 120 grams

1 c of granulated sugar = 200 grams

1 c of powdered sugar = 120 grams

1 c of brown sugar = 220 grams

1 cup of milk = 240 milliliters

1 cup of heavy cream = 240 milliliters

1 cup of yogurt = 240 grams

CONCLUSION

Thank you for joining me on this culinary journey through the world of vegan delights using the Ninja Creami Deluxe. It's been a pleasure to share these recipes, each crafted to bring out the best in plant-based ingredients and make the most of this innovative kitchen appliance.

I hope these recipes have inspired you to experiment, create, and enjoy delicious, frozen desserts and add more plant-based treats to your diet.

Made in the USA
Las Vegas, NV
01 November 2024

10859426R00044